Sleeping Animals

Written by Sarah O'Neil
Photography by Michael Curtain

This is a bird.

It is sleeping on a branch.
It is sleeping with its head
under its wing.

This is a lizard.

It is sleeping on a branch.
It is sleeping hanging on.

This is a snake.
It is sleeping on a branch.

It is sleeping curled up.

This is a shark.
It is sleeping in the sea.
It is sleeping as it swims.

This is a fish.
It is sleeping in water.
It is sleeping with its eyes open.

This is a butterfly.
It is sleeping on a flower.
It is sleeping with its wings up.

This is a moth.
It is sleeping on a rock.
It is sleeping with its wings down.

This is a tiger.
It is sleeping on the ground.
It is sleeping lying down.

This is a koala.
It is sleeping on a branch.
It is sleeping curled up.

This is a bat.
It is sleeping in a tree.
It is sleeping upside down.

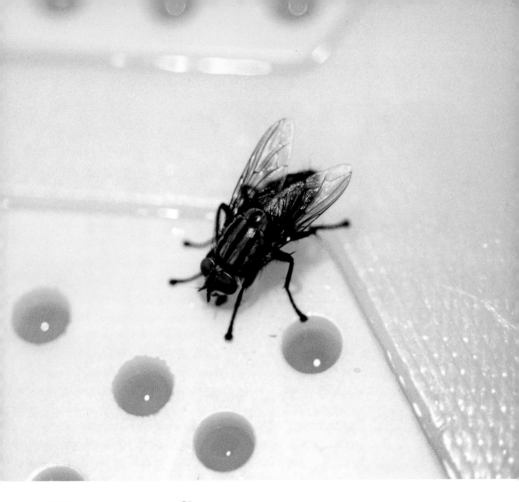

This is a fly.
A fly can sleep anywhere.
It is sleeping standing up.

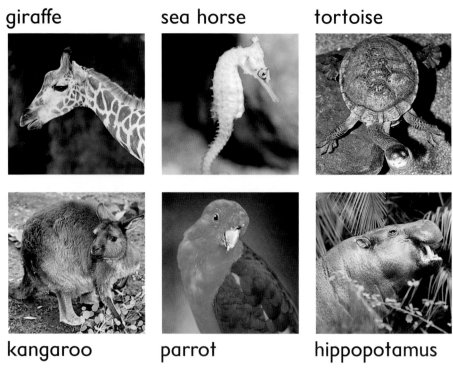

giraffe

sea horse

tortoise

kangaroo

parrot

hippopotamus

All animals sleep.
They sleep in different places.
They sleep in different ways.
How do you think these
animals sleep?